Peaceful Solo Piano Christmas 2

Louis Landon
solo piano sheet music

Bio:
Louis Landon is a composer and Steinway Artist, formerly of New York and currently of Sedona, who has dedicated his life to music. His passion is for peace. His career has taken him around the world playing a variety of styles with some of the mostrecognized names in the entertainment industry: classical music for Mikhail Baryshnikov on national and international tours, Latin music with "Pucho and his Latin Soul Brothers" on national and international tours, pop music with Rupert "Pina Colada Song" Holmes on television and national tours, rock & roll with John Hall, opening for "Little Feat" on national tours. For the past 28 years, through his production company, Landon Music Company, he has written and produced music for film, video, and commercials, including three years of "best plays" and "bloopers" commercials for the National Basketball Association.

Not long ago, Landon realized that his music - the solo piano compositions that bring him so much joy and peace, could surely bring joy, and particularly peace, to millions around the world. Louis Landon is currently working with three missions:
1. To create a more loving and peaceful world by writing, recording and performing, music from the heart.
2. To inspire people to live joyously and passionately.
3. To awaken and to assist people in healing themselves through music and mentoring.

He has released 24 CDs on the LCI record label, his latest entitled *Classic Pop Rock Solo Piano*, was released on July 1, 2017. He is currently working on *Peaceful Solo Piano Christmas 2,* with a release date of November 1, 2017.

Reviews:
"He has a gift for composition that is second to none."
New Age Reporter

"…for those who like their solo piano music rich and full."
Wind & Wire

"… indeed meditative and mellow, [he] sacrifices no musical rigor to achieve those ends. With backgrounds in jazz, Latin music, rock, pop, film composing, and classical piano, Louis brings his breadth and depth of experience to bear here. His playing and compositions are sensitive as they are complex and… a diverse range of influences is more than apparent."
Keyboard Magazine

"While some pianists are virtuosos in their playing and others may not be as technically proficient but have great emotional content in their music, Louis Landon brings it all together with impeccable style and grace. His work covers diverse compositional terrain, incorporating influences of classical, new age, jazz, pop, and more in a mellifluous spectrum of moods and musical colors."
Michaeldiamondmusic.com

Awards and Facts:
Louis landon's music has had over 92 million plays on Pandora radio!

Healing Hearts 2 – Solo Piano won album of the year, 2016, at solopiano.com.

Healing Hearts - Solo Piano was nominated for album of the year, 2015, at Whisperings Radio.

Solo Piano for Love, Peace & Mermaids was nominated for album of the year, 2010, at Whisperings Radio.

Solo Piano for Peace was nominated for the 2009 zmr music awards in three categories: album of the year, best instrumental album - piano, and best cover art by Zone Music Reporter. Solo Piano for Peace was listed at #30 of the top 100 albums for airplay in 2009 by Zone Music Reporter.

Peace Revolution! was louis landon's 7th CD and 2nd solo piano CD. It was #7 on the NAR top 100 charts and was played on over 50 stations worldwide.

unwind charted at #3 of the top 100 cds for the month of February, 2006 on newagereporter.com's website, playing on over 121 stations internationally.

ISBN: 978-0-9863062-9-7
©2017 Landon Creative, Inc

Peaceful Solo Piano Christmas 2
sheet music for solo piano
Louis Landon

Table of contents

Hark! The Herald Angel Sings	1
O Come, All Ye Faithful	5
We Wish You a Merry Christmas	8
Angels We Have Heard on High	11
My Joyous Christmas Soul	15
O Come, O Come Emmanuel	24
It Came Upon a Midnight Clear	31
Here We Come A-Caroling	35
Away in a Manger	36
Good King Wenceslas	39
O Little Town of Bethlehem	41
I Saw Three Ships	44
Christmas Bells	49
We Three Kings	53

Hark! The Herald Angels Sing

from the solo piano CD *Peaceful Solo Piano Christmas 2*
Available from www.louislandon.com

TRADITIONAL
arr. LOUIS LANDON

With feeling ♩ = 80

Copyright © 2017 Landon Creative, Inc. (BMI)
International Copyright Secured. All Rights Reserved.

Hark! The Herald Angels Sing, Louis Landon

A little faster ♩ = 124

louislandon.com　　　　　　　　　　　　　　　　　　　　　　　　*Hark! The Herald Angels Sing*, Louis Landon

O Come, All Ye Faithful

from the solo piano CD *Peaceful Solo Piano Christmas 2*
Available from www.louislandon.com

TRADITIONAL
arr. LOUIS LANDON

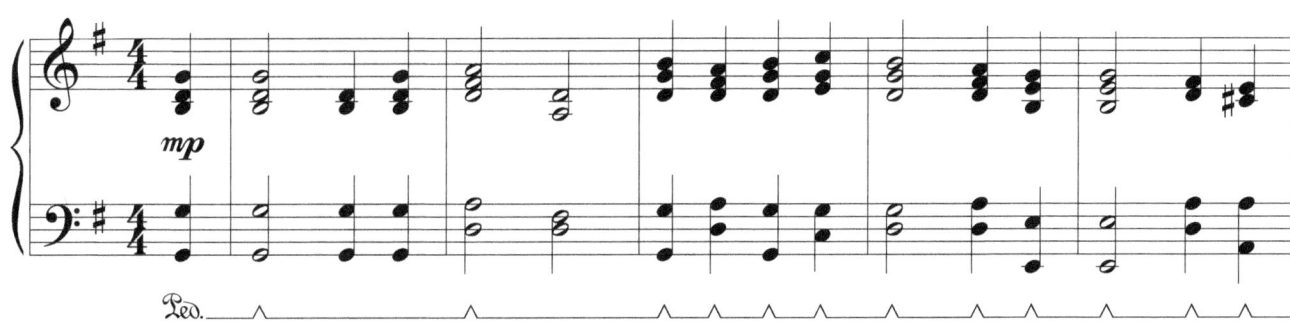

Copyright © 2017 Landon Creative, Inc. (BMI)
International Copyright Secured. All Rights Reserved.

louislandon.com

O Come, All Ye Faithful, Louis Landon

A little faster ♩= 134

O Come, All Ye Faithful, Louis Landon

We Wish You a Merry Christmas

from the solo piano CD *Peaceful Solo Piano Christmas 2*
Available from www.louislandon.com

TRADITIONAL
arr. LOUIS LANDON

Copyright © 2017 Landon Creative, Inc. (BMI)
International Copyright Secured. All Rights Reserved.

louislandon.com — We Wish You a Merry Christmas, Louis Landon

We Wish You a Merry Christmas, Louis Landon

Angels We Have Heard on High

from the solo piano CD *Peaceful Solo Piano Christmas 2*
Available from *www.louislandon.com*

TRADITIONAL
arr. LOUIS LANDON

Copyright © 2017 Landon Creative, Inc. (BMI)
International Copyright Secured. All Rights Reserved.

Angels We Have Heard on High, Louis Landon

My Joyous Christmas Soul

from the solo piano CD *Peaceful Solo Piano Christmas 2*
Available from *www.louislandon.com*

LOUIS LANDON

Sparkling ♩ = 86

Copyright © 2017 Landon Creative, Inc. (BMI)
International Copyright Secured. All Rights Reserved.

My Joyous Christmas Soul, Louis Landon

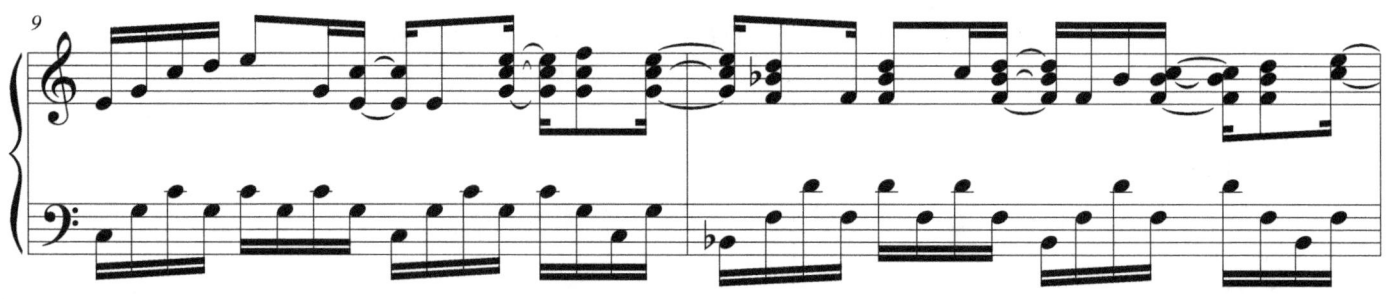

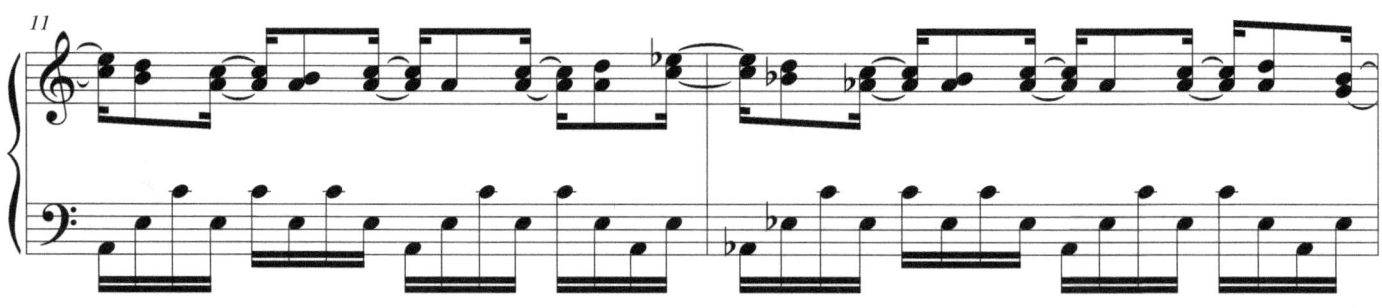

louislandon.com

My Joyous Christmas Soul, Louis Landon

louislandon.com

My Joyous Christmas Soul, Louis Landon

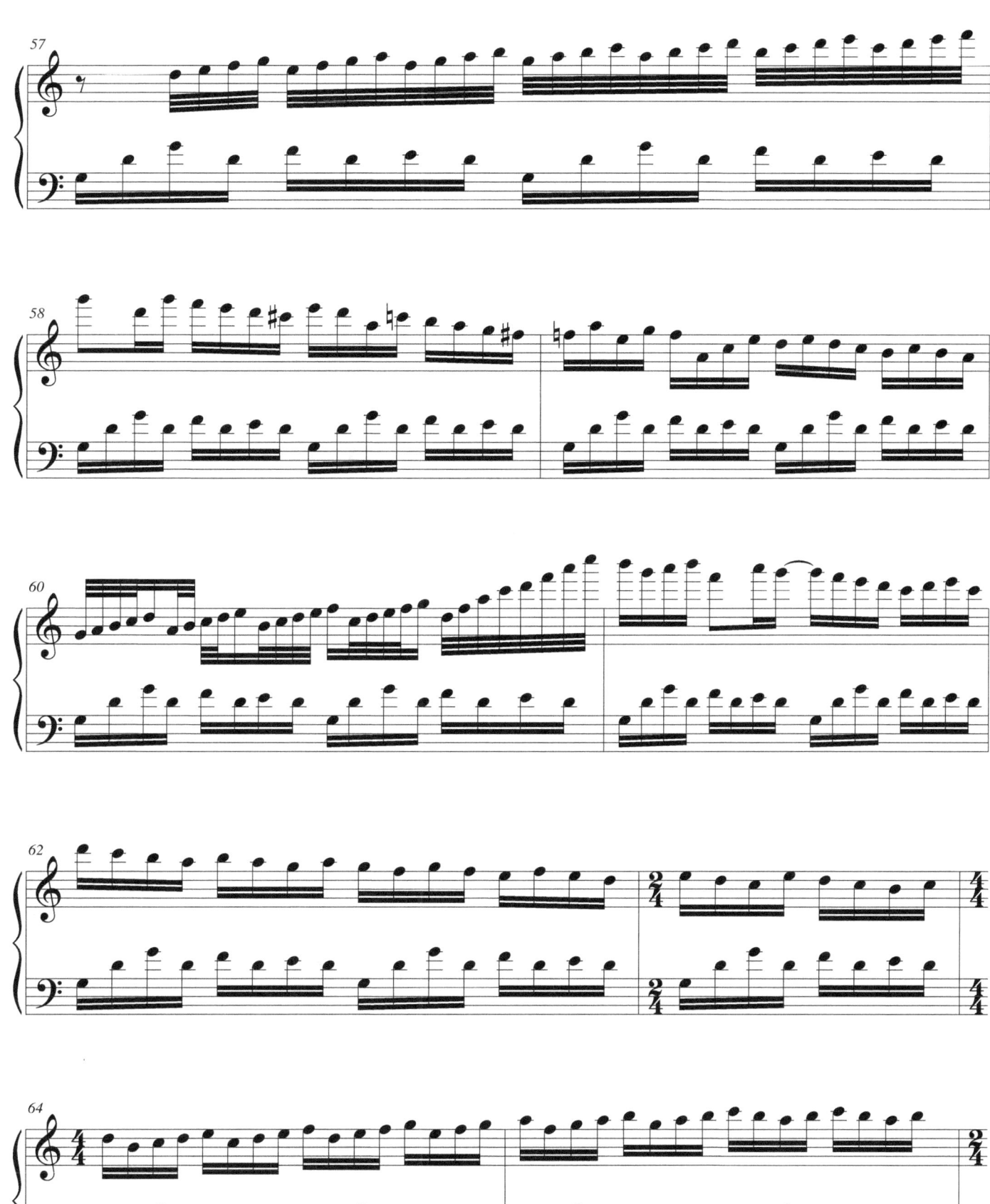

My Joyous Christmas Soul, Louis Landon

O Come, O Come Emmanuel

from the solo piano CD *Peaceful Solo Piano Christmas 2*
Available from www.louislandon.com

TRADITIONAL
arr. LOUIS LANDON

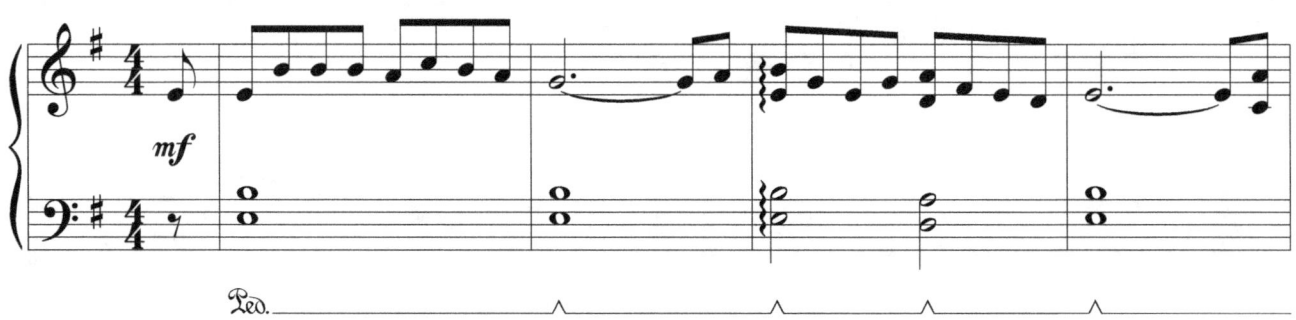

Copyright © 2017 Landon Creative, Inc. (BMI)
International Copyright Secured. All Rights Reserved.

louislandon.com *O Come, O Come Emmanuel*, Louis Landon

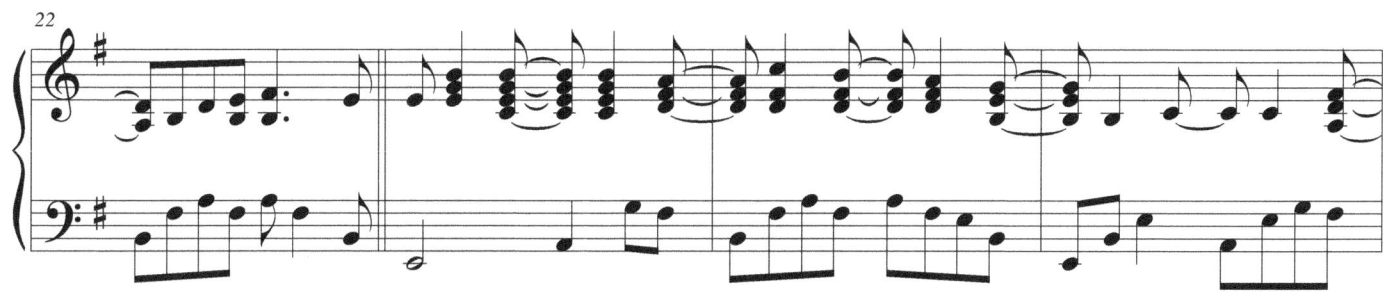
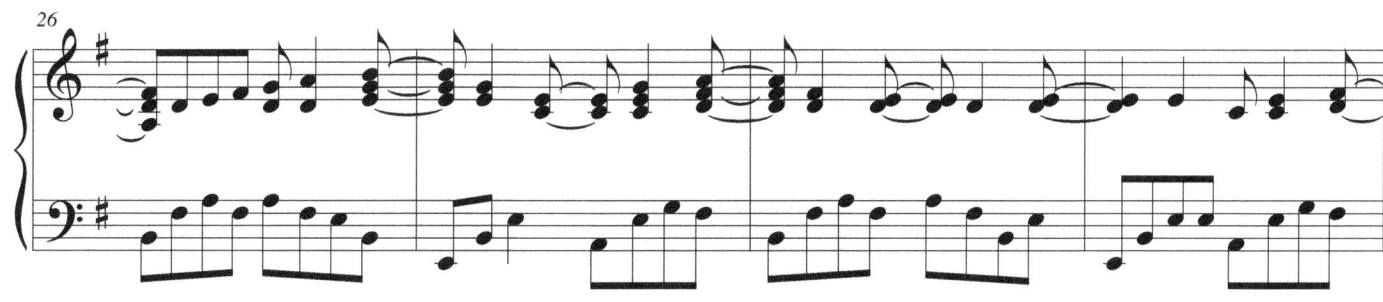

O Come, O Come Emmanuel, Louis Landon

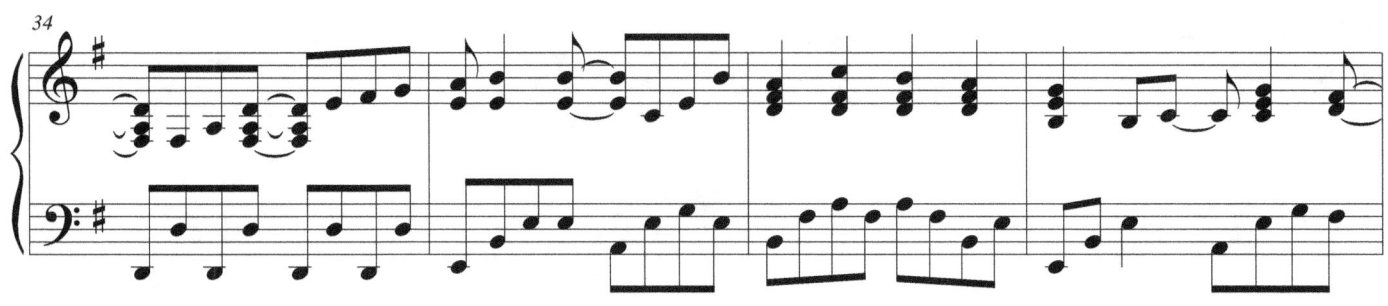
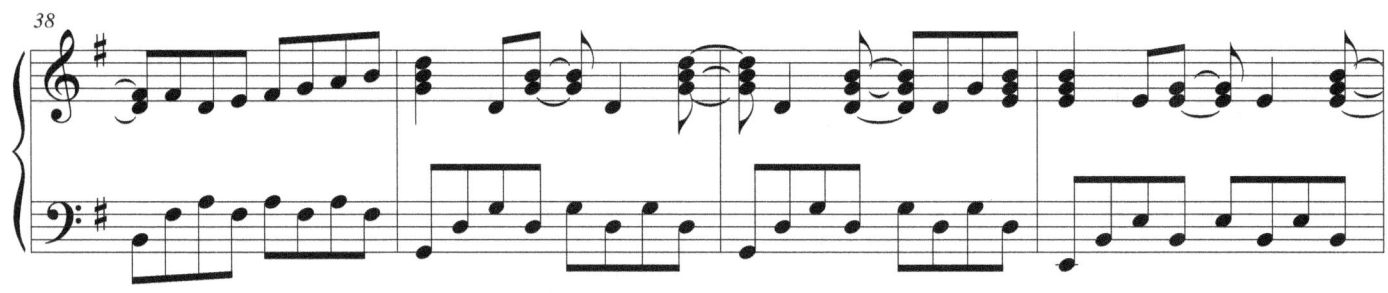

O Come, O Come Emmanuel, Louis Landon

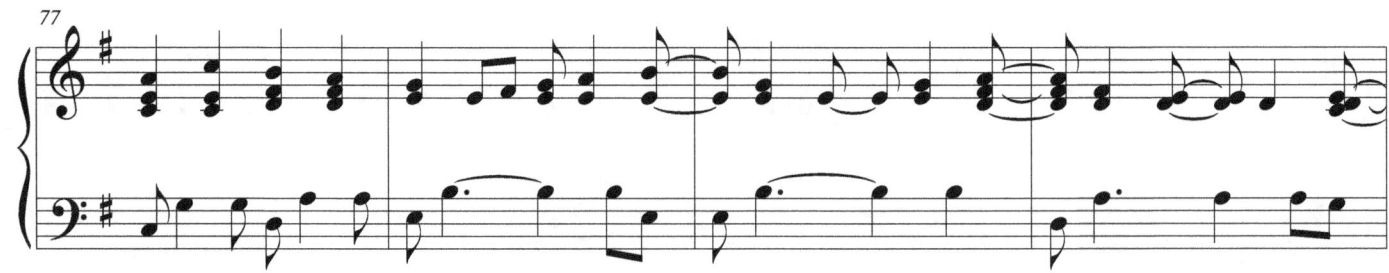

29

louislandon.com *O Come, O Come Emmanuel*, Louis Landon

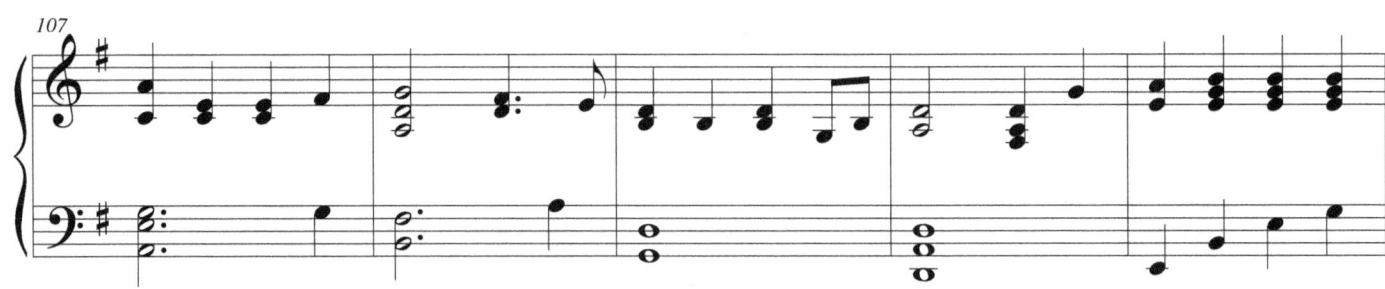
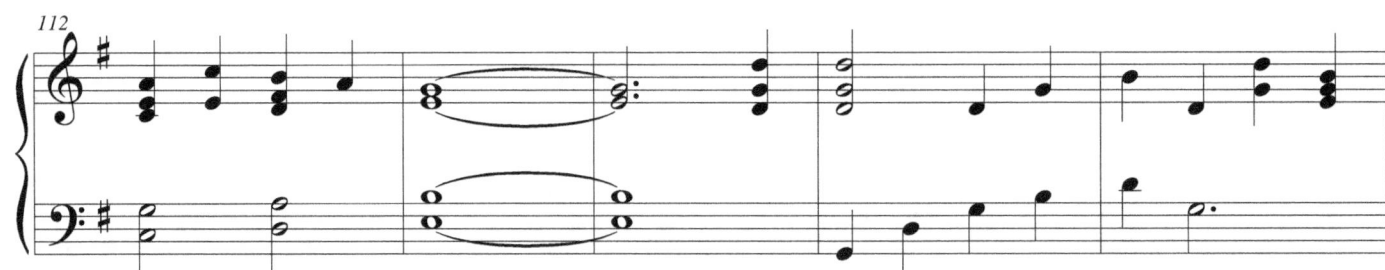

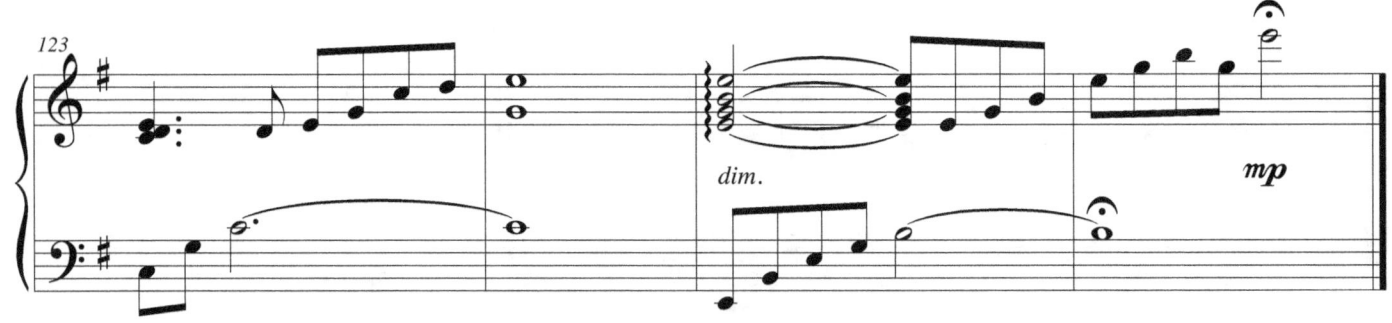

It Came Upon a Midnight Clear

from the solo piano CD *Peaceful Solo Piano Christmas 2*
Available from *www.louislandon.com*

TRADITIONAL
arr. LOUIS LANDON

It Came Upon a Midnight Clear, Louis Landon

Here We Come A-Caroling

from the solo piano CD *Peaceful Solo Piano Christmas 2*
Available from www.louislandon.com

TRADITIONAL
arr. LOUIS LANDON

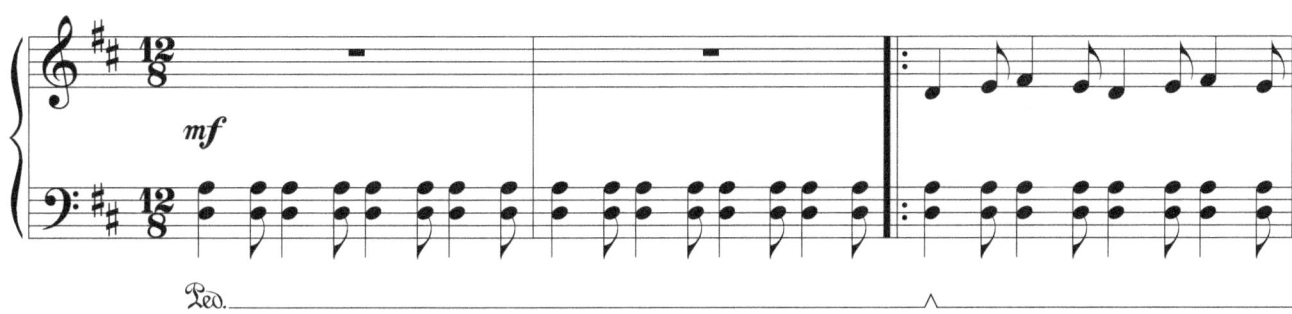

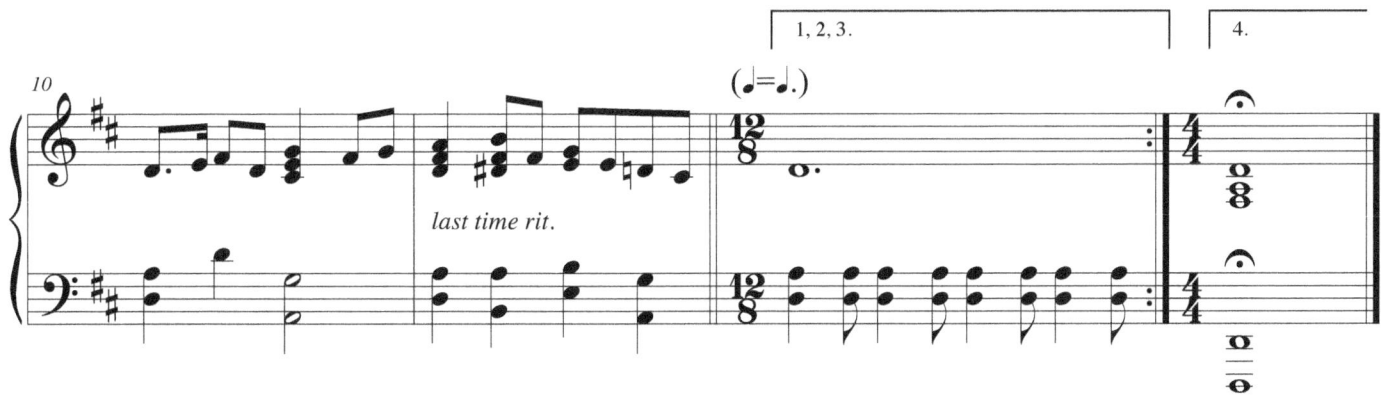

Copyright © 2017 Landon Creative, Inc. (BMI)
International Copyright Secured. All Rights Reserved.

Away in a Manger

from the solo piano CD *Peaceful Solo Piano Christmas 2*
Available from *www.louislandon.com*

TRADITIONAL
arr. LOUIS LANDON

Copyright © 2017 Landon Creative, Inc. (BMI)
International Copyright Secured. All Rights Reserved.

Away in a Manger, Louis Landon

Good King Wenceslas

from the solo piano CD *Peaceful Solo Piano Christmas 2*
Available from *www.louislandon.com*

TRADITIONAL
arr. LOUIS LANDON

Copyright © 2017 Landon Creative, Inc. (BMI)
International Copyright Secured. All Rights Reserved.

O Little Town of Bethlehem

from the solo piano CD *Peaceful Solo Piano Christmas 2*
Available from www.louislandon.com

TRADITIONAL
arr. LOUIS LANDON

Sweetly ♩ = 100

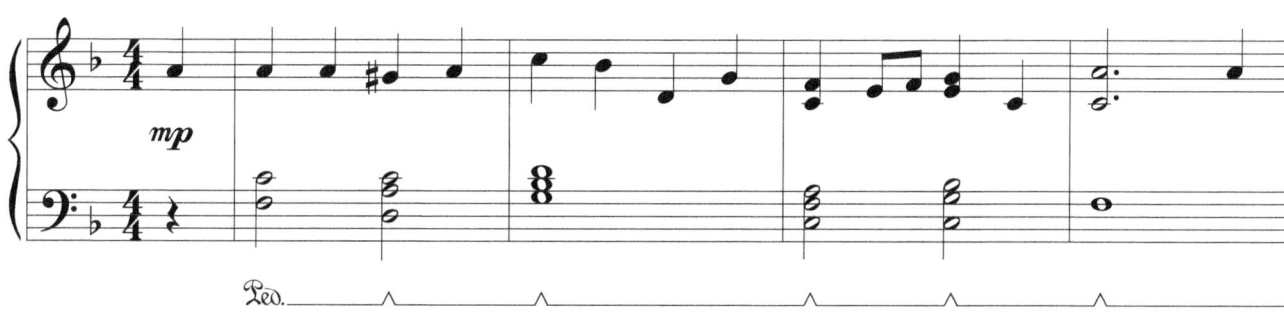

Copyright © 2017 Landon Creative, Inc. (BMI)
International Copyright Secured. All Rights Reserved.

O Little Town of Bethlehem, Louis Landon

I Saw Three Ships

from the solo piano CD *Peaceful Solo Piano Christmas 2*
Available from *www.louislandon.com*

TRADITIONAL
arr. LOUIS LANDON

Spirited ♩. = 128

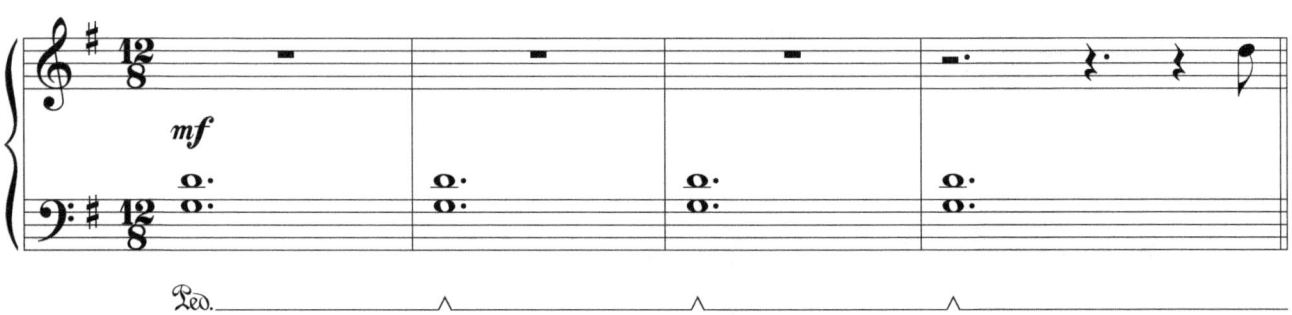

Copyright © 2017 Landon Creative, Inc. (BMI)
International Copyright Secured. All Rights Reserved.

louislandon.com *I Saw Three Ships*, Louis Landon

louislandon.com

I Saw Three Ships, Louis Landon

I Saw Three Ships, Louis Landon

Christmas Bells

from the solo piano CD *Peaceful Solo Piano Christmas 2*
Available from *www.louislandon.com*

LOUIS LANDON

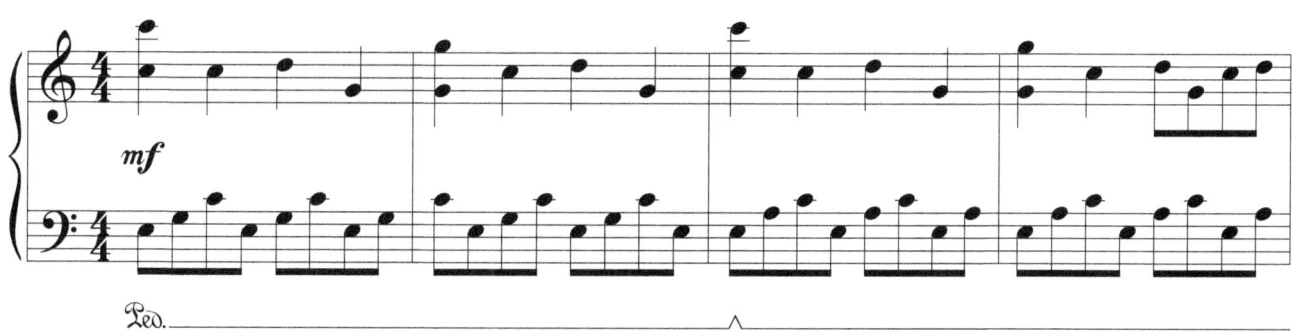

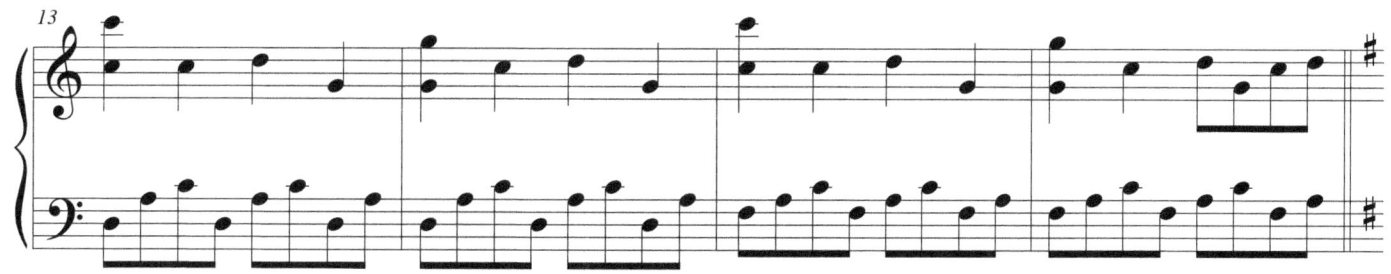

Christmas Bells, Louis Landon

We Three Kings

from the solo piano CD *Peaceful Solo Piano Christmas 2*
Available from www.louislandon.com

TRADITIONAL
arr. LOUIS LANDON

Copyright © 2017 Landon Creative, Inc. (BMI)
International Copyright Secured. All Rights Reserved.

louislandon.com

We Three Kings, Louis Landon

ISBN 978-0-9863062-9-7

www.ingramcontent.com/pod-product-compliance
Lightning Source LLC
Chambersburg PA
CBHW080554230426
43663CB00015B/2830